😃 theoloji 101 🙏

Catholic Theology + Emojis

jared ✍ dees

© 2025 by Jared Dees

All rights reserved.

No part of this book may be reproduced or used in any manner without written permission from the copyright owner, except for the use of quotations in a book review.

For more information, visit jareddees.com.

Paperback: ISBN 978-1-954135-16-1
eBook: ISBN 978-1-954135-17-8

contents

😊 Theology + Emoji = Theoloji	v
1. 🤭 God 🤭	1
2. 🖐 Divine Revelation 🖐	5
3. 📖 Bible 📖	7
4. ☘ Trinity ☘	11
5. ✝ Christology ✝	15
6. 🕊 Holy Spirit 🕊	19
7. 💾 Salvation, Sin, and Grace 💾	23
8. 😇 Soteriology 😈	27
9. ⛪ Ecclesiology ⛪	31
10. 👑 Mariology 👑	35
11. ✝ Sacraments ✝	39
12. 🙏 Prayer 🙏	47
13. ✅ Morality ✅	53
14. 🙌 Commandments 🙌	57
15. 😂 Beatitudes 😂	61
16. 💚 Virtues 💚	65
17. ⚖ Catholic Social Teaching ⚖	69
18. 📅 Liturgical Year 📅	73
✍ Author's Note	85
🤖 About the Author	87
📚 Also by Jared Dees	89
🤓 About TheReligionTeacher.com	91

😃 theology + emoji = theoloji

😃 The word "emoji" comes from the Japanese words for picture (e) and character (moji).

Emojis are picture-words.

Like emoticons (emotion + icons), emojis express ideas and emotions in images.

😇📖 what is theology?

Theo = "God"

logy = "the study of"

Theology literally means "the study of God."

But for the Christian, God is more than a subject of study.

A more accurate goal for theology, according to St. Anselm, is:

🔭 "Faith seeking understanding."

. . .

Does God exist?

Yes, and we can prove it!

At least, that is what St. Thomas Aquinas did with his Five Proofs of God:

☞ The First Mover

🎆 Causation

∞ Contingency

☝ Degree

🏁 Final End

☞ the first mover

Everything can move.

Everything that moves was moved by something else.

Something must have been the first mover.

God was the first mover.

✏️ causation

Nothing causes itself to exist.

Without our parents, we don't exist.

Without their parents, they don't exist.

What existed first?

The first cause: God.

∞ contingency

Something either exists or not.

There was a time when something that exists didn't exist yet.

What existed before all things existed?

All that exists is contingent upon that which always existed: God.

👌 degree

We can compare things by degrees of perfection.

Some things are more perfect than others.

A circle, for example, can be drawn more perfectly round than another circle.

What would be the most perfect of all?

God is absolute perfection.

🥅 final end

Everything has a goal.

Why?

What tells a plant to grow or an animal to eat?

What tells the planet to spin?

There must be some intelligence behind all these ends.

God gives the goals.

God directs the final end.

🙌 divine revelation 🙌

. . .

We can accept that God exists through reason, but we can also know about him through Divine Revelation.

🙌 Divine Revelation = God reveals himself to his people.

📖 The story of that revelation is recorded in the Bible.

God revealed himself through various stages described in the Bible, particularly:

🍎 Adam and Eve

🐏 Noah

👫 Patriarchs

👥 Moses & the People of Israel

✝️ Jesus Christ

After Jesus, there will be no further Divine Revelation.

🤝 the covenants 🤝

God made covenants with his people over time.

Covenants are like holy, unbreakable contracts.

God made covenants with:

📜 Noah

👫 Abraham

🙌 Moses

👑 David

Then:

✝️ Jesus Christ brought the New and Final Covenant.

There will be no more Divine Revelation.

🙏 can people experience private revelations from god?

Yes. Private revelations in prayer, dreams, or visions can certainly lead people closer to Christ.

But these revelations cannot add to or change God's final revelation in Jesus Christ.

📖 bible 📖

· · ·

The word Bible actually means "books." The Bible is a collection of many books.

It is also called Scripture, which comes from the Latin word for "writings."

The Bible is a collection of many books divinely inspired by God and written by human hands.

☞

🤝 what does testament mean?

The Bible is divided into two parts:

✡ Old Testament

✝ New Testament

Testament is another word for "Covenant."

🏛 Old Testament = God's covenant with Israel

⛪ New Testament = God's covenant through Christ with the Church

📚 the books of the bible 📚

Old Testament

✋ The Pentateuch ("5 Books") or Torah

👑 The Historical Books

✍ Novellas

🤔 Wisdom Books

😲 Prophets

New Testament

📖 Gospels (and Acts)

✉ St. Paul's Letters

✉ Catholic Letters

☁ Revelation

📖 how to read the bible 📖

The Senses of Scripture

🍵 ♂ Literal = What does it say?

✋ Spiritual = What does it say to me?

👇 Which includes:

🔀 Allegorical: What is the connection between the Old Testament and Jesus Christ?

☺ Moral: How should I act?

😇 Anagogical: How does this lead me to heaven?

⌛ salvation history in 15 emojis ⌛

God revealed his saving plan for humanity beginning with Creation and ending with Christ.

1. 🌍
2. 🐍
3. 🌈
4. 🧔
5. 🆓
6. 🔟
7. 🫅
8. 🏰
9. 🗣
10. 👋
11. 👶
12. ✝️
13. 🌄
14. ☁️
15. 🔥

⌛ salvation history in 15 emojis (explained) ⌛

1. 🌍 Creation

2. 🐍 Fall

3. 🚢 Covenant with Noah

4. 👴 Patriarchs

5. 🆓 Freedom from Egypt

6. 🔟 Covenant and Ten Commandments

7. 🧑‍⚖️ Judges

8. 👑 King and Davidic Covenant

9. 🗣 Prophets

10. ⛓ Babylonian Captivity

11. 👶 Christ was Born

12. ✝️ Christ Died

13. 🌅 Christ Rose Again

14. ☁️ Christ Ascended to Heaven

15. 🔥 Christ Gives the Holy Spirit to the Church

☘ trinity ☘

· · ·

There is only one God, but God revealed himself as a Holy Trinity of three persons.

God is:

🚶 Father

👶 Son

🕊 Holy Spirit

🔍 the holy trinity is a mystery

🫖 It isn't a mystery like a problem to be solved. No answer can perfectly express the Trinity.

😇 God reveals himself in the mystery of the Trinity, and theology helps us continuously grow in our understanding of God.

📖 God's revelation as a Trinity is recorded in the New Testament.

✝ "In the beginning was the Word, and the Word was with God, and the Word was God." (Jn 1:1)

🧬 Jesus told his disciples to baptize "in the name of the Father and of the Son and of the Holy Spirit." (Mt 28:19)

📇 trinity terminology

The Church borrowed some terms from philosophy to explain the mystery of the Trinity:

♾ Substance: God is one being, essence, or nature.

🔄 Consubstantial: The Son and Father are one substance.

🚹 Person: God is distinctly three and in relationship with each other.

🔥 🕊 the holy spirit

The Holy Spirit proceeds from the Father and the Son.

🕊 The Holy Spirit came upon Jesus in the form of a dove at his baptism.

🔥 The Holy Sprit came upon the Apostles as tongues of fire on Pentecost.

⛪ The Holy Spirit continues to be with the Church today.

👀 trinity symbols

Many symbols have been used to express the mystery of the Trinity (one God, three persons).

Trinity Emojis:

☻ Theoloji 101 🙏

☘ Shamrock: three leaves, one stem

♣ Trefoil: three leaves, one plant

⚜ Fleur-de-Lis: tree petals, one stem

▲ Triangle: three sides, one shape

✝ christology ✝

. . .

Christology is the theology of Jesus Christ, human and divine.

How can Jesus be both human and divine?

This is THE question in Christology.

✝ what is jesus christ's nature?

🔁 Jesus is consubstantial (one substance) with the Father. Jesus is divine. He is God.

🧍 Jesus is also a human person. He became a man like us in all but sin.

These are not two natures but one nature.

🤘 the hypostatic union 🤘

The Greek philosophical term "hypostasis" refers to the fundamental reality of something.

The fundamental reality of Christ:

👆 One Jesus = 😊 human & 😇 divine

✖ heresies ✖

False Christologies:

🦅 Arianism: Jesus wasn't God but is eternal

😵 Docetism: Jesus was God and only appeared to be human

👥 Nestorianism: Jesus had two natures (human and divine)

😇 Monophysitism: Jesus's divinity canceled out his humanity

👑 15 names and titles of jesus christ and their meanings

1. 💾 Jesus = "God saves"

2. 😇 Christ = "Messiah" = "Anointed One"

3. ✌ Emmanuel = "God is with us"

4. 🙏 Lord = God, title used instead of God's name

5. 👨‍🏫 Rabbi = Teacher

6. 🗣 Word = Logos = Jesus is Divine

7. 👼 Son of God = Jesus is Divine

8. 🙂 Son of Man = Jesus is human (not just God) and will come again to judge the world

9. ♚ Son of David = Jesus is an heir of King David, Jesus is the Messiah

10. 👑 King of the Jews = Jesus is the Messiah

11. 🐑 Lamb of God = Jesus is the sacrificial lamb that died for our sins

12. 🔖 Redeemer = Jesus "buys back" our salvation & frees from sin

13. 🚶 New Adam = Through Adam's disobedience came sin and death, but through Christ's obedience comes grace and life

14. 💡 Light of the World = Jesus is light in the darkness of this world

15. 🍞 Bread of Life = Jesus is the bread from heaven to give everlasting life, similar to the manna from heaven in the Old Testament

holy spirit

...

what is the holy spirit?

⏩ The Holy Spirit is Divine. It is consubstantial with the Father and Son. It is one of the three persons of the Trinity.

↔ The Holy Spirit proceeds from the Father and Son.

the meaning of holy spirit

🙏 Holy = Divine, of God

💨 Spirit = Hebrew word "ruah" means "air, breath, or wind".

Like air or wind, we cannot see the Spirit of God, but it is here with us.

the paraclete or advocate

Jesus called the Holy Spirit the Advocate or Paraclete,

which means literally "to call beside us" and also "helper," "consoler," or "lawyer" (Jn 14).

We can turn to the Holy Spirit to help us follow God's Law.

👀 the symbols of the holy spirit

🕊 The Holy Spirit came upon Jesus in the form of a dove after his baptism.

🔥 The Holy Spirit came upon the Apostles as tongues of fire on Pentecost.

🫁 Jesus breathed on the Apostles to give them the Holy Spirit, similar to how God's breath gave Adam life in the Creation story.

💧 We receive the Holy Spirit through the waters of Baptism.

🫙 We are anointed with oil in Confirmation to be sealed with the Holy Spirit.

☞ God wrote the Ten Commandments on the tablets with his finger. God sends the Holy Spirit to write the Law on our hearts.

✋ The power of the Holy Spirit to heal and bless is bestowed especially in the sacraments through hands.

🎁 the 7 gifts of the holy spirit

🤔 Wisdom

👍 Understanding

🤓 Knowledge

👻 Counsel

💪 Fortitude

🙏 Piety

😮 Fear of the Lord

(Isaiah 11:2-3)

🍇 the fruits of the holy spirit

😍 love (charity)

🥰 joy

☺️ peace

🙂 patience

🥰 kindness

🤩 generosity

🤗 faithfulness

☺️ gentleness

🤫 self-control

(Galatians 5:22–23)

💾 salvation, sin, and grace 💾

. . .

What is salvation, and why do we need it?

Here is an introduction to:

💾 Salvation

👀 Justification

☺ Sin

🎁 Grace

👇

💾 names for salvation

💾 Saved: We are saved from sin (separation from God) and given eternal life with the Lord

📖 Redemption: Jesus "bought back" our salvation & frees us from sin

👀 Justification: The grace of God cleanses us from our sins and invites us to righteousness

👀 how justification works

↪ Moved by grace, we turn to God and away from sin

🔟 We accept forgiveness and righteousness (justice) from God

⬆ We enter in the process of sanctification and renewal

How?

✝ The Passion of Christ merited our justification

😔 sin

what is sin?

🏹 Sin (*cheit* in Hebrew) literally means "missing the mark," an offense against God

🍎 original sin

1) First Sin

2) Our fallen state of separation from God & tendency toward sin

💀 mortal sin & 🤕 venial sin

💀 Mortal Sin: separates us from God

🤕 Venial Sin: hurts our relationship with God

💀 mortal sin

💟 To destroy the charity of God in our hearts, a mortal sin must meet three conditions:

1) 🎯 Grave Matter: we commit a serious act

2) 🤔 Full Knowledge: we know it is wrong

3) 🤝 Complete Consent: we freely choose to do it

🎁 grace

💝 Grace is a free and undeserved gift of God's life to become his children

😇 Sanctifying Grace is the habitual gift of God's life and love

👻 Actual Grace is God's love at work in specific moments

✝ salvation through jesus christ:

💀 Sin leads to death and separation from God

✝ Although sinless, Christ died and rose to life again

😇 Through Baptism, we die to our sin and rise to new life in Christ

⛅ We are made holy on earth and gain eternal life in heaven

😇 soteriology 👿

. . .

what happens to us after we die?

Soteriology is the theology of salvation and the afterlife.

Here is an introduction to:

- 🌄 The Resurrection
- 💀 Christian Death
- 🌿 Heaven
- 😐 Purgatory
- 🔥 Hell
- 🌍 The Last Judgment

🌄 the resurrection

🧍 ✨ We believe in the resurrection of the body and soul.

💀 😇 Just as Jesus Christ died and rose again, those who die with him will rise with him.

💀 what is death?

🧍 ✂️ ✨ Death is the separation of the soul from the body.

⚖️ After death our souls experience the Particular Judgment:

⚖️ the particular judgment

Our souls are judged upon our death and we enter into:

🏡 Heaven

😐 Purgatory

or

🔥 Hell

🏡 heaven 😇

😇 Those who die in a state of perfect grace go immediately to heaven.

☺ Heaven is the experience of perfect joy and happiness.

😊 The Beatific Vision: We will see God face to face.

♾️ We will be in perfect unity with God and the other saints.

😐 purgatory 😇

🧹 Purgatory means "purification." In purgatory the soul is purified on the way to heaven to become perfectly holy.

😇 Everyone in purgatory will go to heaven. Everyone.

Purgatory is the reason we pray for the dead.

hell

Hell is the complete separation from God for those who do not love God.

Those who die in a state of grave separation (mortal sin) from God remain separated from him for eternity.

Jesus referred to the experience of hell as the "unquenchable fire."

the last judgment

Jesus Christ will come again in glory.

He will separate the righteous from the sinners.

Our souls will be reunited with our bodies.

Heaven and earth will be renewed and the Kingdom of God will come into its fullness.

 ecclesiology

Ecclesiology is the theology of the Church.

the church is:

- The People of God
- The Body of Christ
- The Bride of Christ
- A Sacrament of Salvation

the four marks of the church

- One
- Holy
- Catholic
- Apostolic

⛻ the church is the people of god

"Church" is "ecclesia" in Latin ("ekklesia" in Greek), which means "called out."

🌐 The Church is a people called out of the world by God.

⛪ Church can refer to the entire People of God, but also a liturgical assembly or place of worship.

🚶 the church is the body of christ

St. Paul described the Church as the Body of Christ in his letters.

😀 Christ is the Head

✋ 🦵 We are the one Body with many parts

👰 the church is the bride of christ

👰 St. Paul described the Church as a bride.

🤵 Jesus told parables about himself as a bridegroom.

😍 The love between Christ and the Church is like the love between a bride and groom.

🤝 the church is a sacrament of salvation

7 ▢ We access the seven sacraments through the Church, but the Church itself is also a sacrament.

🔍 A sacrament is the visible sign of invisible grace.

🤝 The Church is the sign of the unity between God and humanity.

✅ the four marks of the church ✅

According to the Creed, we believe in the Church that is:

☝ One

🙏 Holy

☞ Catholic

🤝 Apostolic

☝ the church is one

Just as God is one in three persons, so too is the Church one in many persons.

Many cultures exist within the one Church.

Although there is division, the Church works toward unity.

🙏 the church is holy

We are made into saints by Christ whose body now is the Church.

The Church leads us to holiness.

☞ the church is catholic

"Catholic" means universal.

The mission of the church is Catholic: to go out to the whole world.

🤝 the church is apostolic

The Church began with the Twelve Apostles.

The Apostles appointed bishops as their successors.

Those bishops appointed new bishops to succeed them.

We can trace all of the Church's leadership from one bishop to the next back to the Apostles.

👑 mariology 👑
. . .

Mariology is the theology of the Virgin Mary.

- 👤 Mother of God
- 👰 Virgin Mary
- 🥚 Immaculate Conception
- ⬆️ Assumption
- 🙏 Marian Devotions
- 😃 Marian Apparitions

👤 mary the mother of god

If Jesus was God and man, then was Mary the Mother of God?

📜 Council of Ephesus (431): Yes!

1 ☐ Jesus is 1 person, 2 natures.

💯 Mary is the mother of Jesus, not just his human nature.

♁ Mary is Theotokos (Greek for Mother of God).

👶 the blessed virgin mary

🐑 In the Annunciation, the angel Gabriel appeared to Mary and she conceived her son Jesus by the Holy Spirit.

👪 Joseph was not the biological father of Jesus.

💯 The Virgin Mary maintained her physical virginity perpetually throughout her entire life.

👶 the immaculate conception

Immaculate Conception = Mary *not* Jesus

👪 Conception: Mary was conceived by two human parents.

😇 Immaculate: She was conceived without sin.

🍎 Why? So that Mary did not pass down Original Sin to Jesus.

🍇 Therefore as Jesus is the New Adam, so Mary is the New Eve.

⬆ the assumption of mary

🕊 Jesus ascended body and soul into heaven. Mary was assumed into heaven by her son.

Original Sin ➡ Death of the Body

😇 Mary was born without sin and remained sinless. She was welcomed body and soul into heaven.

🙏 marian devotions

💒 To pray to Mary is to ask her to pray to her Son for us.

🙏 Devotion to Mary is devotion to her Son.

Some popular Marian prayers include:

👐 Hail Mary

💬 Rosary

👼 Angelus/Regina Caeli

👑 Hail, Holy Queen

🫠 Memorare

🤩 marian apparitions

Apparitions are visions of Mary, including Our Lady of:

🇲🇽 Guadalupe

🇫🇷 Lourdes

🇵🇹 Fatima

😇 Her messages through these apparitions helped spread the Christian faith.

🙌 These apparitions were the source of many miracles.

🚶 The locations of the apparitions became holy pilgrimage sites.

✝ sacraments ✝
. . .

The sacraments are visible signs of invisible grace.

7 ▢ the seven sacraments

Here is an introduction to the Seven Sacraments of the Catholic Church:

🫒 Baptism

🕊 Confirmation

🍞 🍷 Eucharist

☺ Reconciliation

☺ Anointing the Sick

👤 👰 Matrimony

☝ Holy Orders

😍 what is a sacrament?

"The sacraments are efficacious signs of invisible grace instituted by Jesus Christ and entrusted to the Church, by which divine life is dispensed to us." (*Catechism of the Catholic Church*, 1131).

🙂 Let's explain:

➡️ The sacraments are efficacious.

They have the power to produce the result or effect of the sacrament.

⚠️ The sacraments are visible signs of invisible grace.

👀 The things we see (water, bread, wine, oil)

🕊 show what we cannot see (grace).

🎁 The sacraments give us grace.

Grace is the free and undeserved gift of God's life.

✝️ The sacraments were instituted by Christ.

Each of the sacraments originates in the life and ministry of Jesus Christ.

. . .

🏛 The sacraments were entrusted to the Church.

The sacraments began with the Apostles and were passed down and are administered through the Church to us today.

😇 The sacraments give us divine life.

We share in the communion of God through the sacraments.

🏛 the seven sacraments are organized into three groups:

🎓 The Sacraments of Initiation

🏢 The Sacraments of Healing

🤝 The Sacraments at the Service of Communion

🎓 the sacraments of initiation

We receive these sacraments to become fully initiated into the Church:

🫗 Baptism

🕊 Confirmation

🍞 🍷 Eucharist

🏥 the sacraments of healing

We receive these sacraments to find healing of body, mind, and soul.

- 😌 Reconciliation
- 🙂 Anointing the Sick

🤝 the sacraments at the service of communion

We receive these sacraments to help others find salvation along with us.

- 👰 🤵 Matrimony
- 🫴 Holy Orders

🔜 an introduction to each of the seven sacraments is coming up next!

💧 baptism 💧

Efficacious Sign:

- 💧 Water

Other symbols:

- 👘 White Garment
- 🕯️ Candle
- 🫙 Chrism Oil

Effects:

😃 Forgiveness of Sin

⛪ Members of the Church

🤝 Unity with Christians

✙ Spiritual Mark of Christ

🕊 confirmation 🕊

Efficacious Signs:

🏺 Oil

🙌 Laying on of the Hands

👁 Seal of the Holy Spirit

Effects:

👼 More Deeply God's Children

✝ Unity with Christ

🎁 Increased Gifts of the Holy Spirit

💪 Strength to Be Witnesses

✙ Spiritual Mark of Christ and the Holy Spirit

🍞 🍷 eucharist 🍞 🍷

Efficacious Signs:

- 🍞 Unleavened Bread
- 🍷 Wine

Effects:

- ✝️ Strengthened Unity with Christ
- ⛪ Unity with the Church
- 🫴 Separation from Venial Sin
- 👀 Commitment to the Poor

😔 reconciliation (penance) 😔

Efficacious Signs:

- 🗣️ Confession, Act of Contrition, and Penance of the Penitent
- ✋ Absolution from the Priest

Effects:

- 😇 Forgiveness of All Sins
- 🙏 Reconciliation with God
- 🤝 Reconciliation with the Church

🤒 anointing of the sick 🤒

Efficacious Signs:

- 🏺 Oil

✋ Laying on of the Hands

Effects:

💪 Strength as a Gift of the Holy Spirit

✝ Unity with Christ in Suffering

⛪ Unity with the Church in Suffering

🏞 Preparation for the Journey to Eternal Life (especially if at the point of death)

👰 🤵 **matrimony** 🤵 👰

Efficacious Sign:

💍 Wedding Vows

Effects:

👰 🤍 💍 🤵 Marital Bond that Lasts Until Death

👰 🤍 🤵 Spouses Help Each Other and Children Attain Holiness

☝ **holy orders** ☝

Efficacious Sign:

✋ Laying on of the Hands

Other Symbols:

- Bishop: Ring, Mitre, Crosier
- Priest: Chrism, Paten, Chalice
- Deacon: Gospels

Effects:

- Priest represents Christ (in persona Christi)
- Priest represents the Church
- Become Priest, Teacher, Pastor

🙏 prayer 🙏
. . .

🙏 the five forms of prayer 🙏

Here is an introduction to the *Catechism of the Catholic Church*'s Five Forms of Prayer:

- 🥺 Petition
- 🙇 Intercession
- 😍 Thanksgiving
- 🤩 Praise
- 😇 Blessing

1. 🥺 prayer of petition

Ask God to help you.

☺ Example: Ask God for forgiveness.

2. 🤗 prayer of intercession

Ask God to help others.

😯 Example: Ask God to heal someone who is sick.

3. 😍 prayer of thanksgiving

Give God gratitude.

😎 Example: Thank God for the beautiful weather.

4. 🤩 prayer of praise

Express God's goodness.

🙌 Example: Praise God for Jesus's great sacrifice on the cross.

5. 😇 prayer of blessing and adoration

Invoke God's grace.

😊 Example: Bless food before eating dinner.

🛐 the three expressions of prayer 🛐

What does prayer look like?

There are three ways to express prayer according to the *Catechism of the Catholic Church*:

😯 Vocal Prayer

🤔 Meditation

😍 Contemplative Prayer

😶 vocal prayer

Vocal prayer is exactly as it sounds.

We pray to God with words (mentally or out loud).

Examples:

The Lord's Prayer (Our Father)

Spontaneous Prayers

🤔 meditation

Meditation is prayerful reflection.

We reflect on the way Christ is working and wants to work in our lives.

We can use . . .

📖 Scripture

📚 Spiritual Books

😇 Writings of the Saints

🖼 Icons & Holy Art

🌍 Nature

...to engage our minds and hearts.

🤔 two common forms of meditation:

📖 Lectio Divina (Sacred Reading)

A sacred reading of the Bible:

📖 Read: What does it say?

🤔 Meditate: What is God saying to me?

🙏 Pray: What can I say in response?

😇 Contemplate: What should I change with God's help?

📿 Rosary

🙏 1 Mystery of Christ's Life = 1 decade (10 Hail Mary's)

🙏 5 Mysteries = 5 decades

🙏 Meditate on the mysteries while you pray.

😍 contemplative prayer

Be in the Lord's presence.

St. Teresa of Avila called it "a close sharing between friends" and "taking time frequently to be alone with him who loves us."

🤔 vs. 😍

In contemplative prayer we can still meditate, but the focus is more on Jesus than our lives.

Meditation isn't always possible, but you can practice contemplative prayer in just moments.

Here are some simple tips:

🧍 Be humble.

💟 Open up the heart.

✝️ Turn to Jesus.

👀 contemplation is seeing

It is a gaze of faith, fixed on Jesus.

"I look at him and he looks at me." —St. John Vianney

👂 contemplation is hearing

Listen to the Word of God and accept it with humble obedience.

🤫 contemplation is silence

Words can be like kindling of the fire of love, but they are not necessary.

Lose yourself in the silence of prayer and let yourself be loved by God.

✅ morality ✅

. . .

God created us in his image and likeness with the free will to choose good and avoid evil.

Here is an introduction to Christian morality:

✅ Human Acts

🫠 Conscience

😵 Passions

☺ Sin

🫡 Law

🫶 Virtues

✅ morality of human acts

What makes an act morally good or evil?

Object + Intention + Circumstances

🕴 Object: What do you want to do?

⚖ Intention: What do you want to happen?

🌐 Circumstances: What conditions are contributing to the decision?

🔍 Case Study: 🏹 Robin Hood

✗ Object: Steal from the rich.

✅ Intention: Give to the poor.

✅ Circumstances: The rich are far richer than the poor.

✗ Immoral Act

The end (intention) does not justify the means (object).

🔍 Case Study: 🏦 Philanthropist

✅ Object: Give to the poor.

✗ Intention: Admiration from rich friends.

✅ Circumstances: A very large donation.

✗ Immoral Act

A bad intention (vanity) makes a good behavior (almsgiving) evil.

🤔 conscience

How can we know if an act is good or evil?

💗 God gave us a conscience.

😊 Theoloji 101 🙏

Our conscience tells us if an act is moral . . .

☜ Before

☟ During

☞ After

. . . an act is performed.

🤔 Conscience Formation

We form our conscience through:

🎓 Education in Virtue

📖 Word of God

😌 Examination of Conscience

🎁 Gifts of the Holy Spirit

👻 Example of Others

⛪ Teachings of the Church

😍 passions

The passions are emotions that lead us to act in a certain way.

😌 Passions are neither good nor evil...until they contribute to good or evil actions.

🏅 Our Goal: Turn passions into virtues, not vices.

🏆 Perfection: Feeling good about doing good.

😌 sin

😌 A morally evil act is a sin.

😔 Sin separates us from God and others.

😄 But God is merciful and ready to offer us forgiveness.

😃☝ god's law

God gives us three kinds of laws:

😌 Natural Law: Everyone is born with the ability to know good and evil.

 Old Law: Ten Commandments

😍 New Law: Love

🫶 Greatest Commandment (Love God and Neighbor)

&

✝️ New Commandment (Love Like Jesus)

🫶 virtues

The virtues are habitual and firm dispositions to do good.

The virtues lead us to perform good acts.

😇

🙌 commandments 🙌

. . .

The Ten Commandments in Emojis:

1. ☝️

2. 🤐

3. 📅

4. 👫

5. 😠

6. 🧍🛡️🍃🧍

7. 👻

8. 😶

9. 🫥

10. 🥺

Continue Reading:

☝ the first commandment

1. I am the LORD your God: you shall not have strange gods before me.

In other words:

🗨 Do not put anyone or anything above God.

🤐 the second commandment

2. You shall not take the name of the LORD your God in vain.

In other words:

💬 Do not curse with God's name.

📅 the third commandment

3. Remember to keep holy the LORD's Day.

In other words:

⛪ Go to church on Sundays.

👨‍👩‍👧 the fourth commandment

4. Honor your father and mother.

In other words:

👨‍👩‍👧 Treat your parents with respect.

😟 the fifth commandment

5. You shall not kill.

In other words:

🗯 Do not murder or even be angry with someone.

😀 🫀 🌿 🙂 the sixth commandment

6. You shall not commit adultery.

In other words:

😶 Do not cheat on your significant other.

👻 the seventh commandment

7. You shall not steal.

In other words:

✊ Do not take something that isn't yours.

👾 the eighth commandment

8. You shall not bear false witness against your neighbor.

In other words:

😬 Do not lie.

👻 the ninth commandment

9. You shall not covet your neighbor's wife.

In other words:

🖤‍🔥 Do not be jealous or desire another person's significant other.

😳 the tenth commandment

10. You shall not covet your neighbor's goods.

In other words:

🤩 Do not be envious of another person's stuff.

😄 beatitudes 😄

. . .

Beatitude means "blessed" or "happy."

😃 the desire for happiness

😃 God gave us all a desire for happiness.

😯 ...but God alone can fulfill our desire for happiness.

😄 The beatitudes show us the path from suffering to happiness in God.

😄 the eight beatitudes

In his Sermon on the Mount, Jesus shared eight Beatitudes to guide his disciples:

1. 👀

2. 😭

3. 😌

4. 😋

5. 🙁

6. 😍

7. 😑

8. 😒

1. 👀 blessed are the poor in spirit, for theirs is the kingdom of heaven.

😍 To be poor in spirit is to love God over money.

😀 Happiness is found in God, not money.

2. 🗣 blessed are those who mourn, for they shall be comforted.

😔 To mourn is to be sad.

🥲 Happiness is found in God who comforts us, not loneliness.

3. 😌 blessed are the meek, for they shall inherit the earth.

😌 To be meek is to be quiet, calm, and gentle.

😎 Happiness is found in God, not arrogance.

4. 😋 blessed are those who hunger and thirst for righteousness, for they shall be satisfied.

😊 To hunger and thirst for righteousness is to seek to be good.

😺 Happiness is found in God who is good, not evil.

5. 😔 blessed are the merciful, for they shall obtain mercy.

🥹 To be merciful is to forgive.

🥲 Happiness is found in God's mercy, not resentment or revenge.

6. 😍 blessed are the pure in heart, for they shall see god.

🐨 To be pure in heart is to love what is holy.

🐵 Happiness is found in God's holiness, not sin.

7. 🫠 blessed are the peacemakers, for they shall be called sons of god.

🐢 To be a peacemaker is to resolve conflicts.

🐸 Happiness is found in God's unity, not division or power.

8. 😣 blessed are those who are persecuted for righteousness' sake, for theirs is the kingdom of heaven.

😬 To be persecuted is to be insulted.

🤩 Happiness is found in God's approval, not the approval of others.

🥳 rejoice and be glad

Jesus concludes the beatitudes with a reminder:

"Rejoice and be glad, for your reward is great in heaven."

😇 Happiness will always be found in heaven.

♡ virtues ♡

· · ·

A virtue is a habitual and firm disposition to do good.

Here is an introduction to the Christian virtues:

☺ Human Virtues

▯ Cardinal Virtues

😇 Theological Virtues

☺ human virtues

Virtues are habits and dispositions of the mind and will that:

🧘 govern our actions and emotions.

🐎 guide our conduct.

♟ enable self-mastery.

👍 allow us to freely practice good actions.

💗 how do we grow in human virtue?

🏫 Education

🏋 Deliberate Practice

🏃 Perseverance

And:

🙏 God's Help

🚪 the cardinal virtues

🚪 "Cardinal" comes from the Latin word for hinge (like a door hinge).

👁 Take away the hinge and everything falls apart.

⛪ All human virtues are grouped into the Cardinal virtues.

🚪 the four cardinal virtues

👉 Prudence (Wisdom)

💪 Fortitude (Courage)

✋ Temperance (Self-control)

🤝 Justice (Fairness)

😇 the theological virtues

✝ These virtues are directly related to God.

❤ They help us grow in our relationship with God.

😇 the three theological virtues:

🤔 Faith (Belief)

🤩 Hope (Trust)

😍 Charity (Love)

⚖️ catholic social teaching ⚖️
...

Here is an introduction to the Church's teachings on social justice:

7 ☐ Seven Principles of Catholic Social Teaching (CST)

🎗 Subsidiarity

🤝 Common Good

7 ☐ the seven principles of cst

👤 Life and Dignity of the Human Person

👪 Call to Family, Community, and Participation

✋ Rights and Responsibilities

👀 Option for the Poor and Vulnerable

👷 The Dignity of Work and the Rights of Workers

✌️ Solidarity

🌍 Care for God's Creation

1. life and dignity of the human person

Meaning:

All life is sacred from conception to death.

Issues:

Abortion, Euthanasia, Cloning, Stem-Cell Research, Death Penalty, Peace

2. call to family, community, and participation

Meaning:

All people have the right to participate in a society that seeks the common good and strengthens communities and families.

Issues:

Marriage and Family Issues

3. rights and responsibilities

Meaning:

We must recognize our duty to society and protect the rights of others.

Issues:

Voting, Volunteering

4. 😟 option for the poor and vulnerable

Meaning:

👉 Put the needs of the poor and vulnerable first.

Issues:

Poverty, Homelessness, Healthcare, Disabilities

5. 👷 the dignity of work and the rights of workers

Meaning:

👷 Everyone should have the opportunity to work. Work adds meaning and motivation to our lives.

Issues:

Discrimination, Just Wages, Unions, Private Property

6. ☝ solidarity

Meaning:

🤝 We are all united as one human family despite our differences.

Issues:

Racism, Discrimination, Peace

7. 🌍 care for god's creation

Meaning:

We must be good stewards of the environment for ourselves and future generations.

Issues:

Pollution, Climate Change

subsidiarity

Nothing should be done at a higher level that can be done well or better at a lower level.

Example:

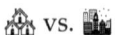

Many decisions are made best in local communities or local governments rather than in the federal government.

the common good

Work toward the greatest good for all persons.

NOT the greatest good for the greatest number of people (or special groups of people).

catholic social teaching conclusion

These principles are just the starting point.

They should inspire us to protect the rights and dignity of all people.

📅 liturgical year 📅

...

⊘ advent ⊘

Advent is a season of preparation for Christmas.

➡️ The word Advent comes from the Latin "ad" (to) and "vent" (come). Advent means "to come." This is because we wait in joyful hope for the coming of Christ in two ways:

🍼 We look forward to Christmas, when we will remember and celebrate the birth of Christ.

✨ We also look forward to the Second Coming of Christ at the end of the world. As Christians we believe Christ will come again!

🎉 happy new year!

📅 The calendar new year begins during the Christmas season on January 1st, but the Church's new year begins on the First Sunday of Advent.

📖 Advent is the first season in the liturgical year and a new cycle of readings begins, featuring one of the three Gospels: Matthew, Mark, or Luke.

🕯 the symbolism of the advent wreath

4 ☐ We light four candles on the Advent wreath to mark the four Sundays we celebrate to prepare for Christmas.

🕯 The light of the candle on the dark days of winter reminds us that Christ is the light of the world.

⬤ Purple is a color to remind us to prepare in prayer and penance for the coming of the Lord.

🌷 Pink (rose) marks the third Sunday of Advent, which is Gaudete Sunday and a reminder of the joy that Christmas is almost here.

🌲 The evergreen wreath from a fir or pine tree, which stays green all year long even through the winter, reminds us of the everlasting life in Christ.

🖼 john the baptist

🖼 John the Baptist is the central figure during Advent because his role in the Gospel was to prepare the way of the Lord. "Make straight a highway for God," he said, echoing the words of the prophet Isaiah.

↩ Repent! His message to repent reminds us to turn toward Jesus as we prepare for Christmas.

🙌 o antiphons

The O Antiphons are a special set of prayers of praise highlighted by the Church at the end of Advent (December 17-24). Each one focuses on a names or a title for Jesus Christ. They might sound familiar from the verses of the Christmas carol "O Come, O Come Emmanuel":

🤔 O Wisdom

👑 O Lord

🌳 O Root of Jesse

🔑 O Key of David

🌅 O Radiant Dawn

🏰 O King of All the Nations

👶 O Emmanuel

🎄 christmas 🎄

👶 Christmas is a celebration of the birth of Christ. The official name for the feast is the "Nativity," which means "arisen from birth."

🎁 We celebrate Jesus's birthday by giving gifts to one another.

🧦 🎵 Stockings hung on the fireplace connect to an old story about St. Nicholas, who gave gold to a family in need in the stockings left by the fireplace to dry.

🎄 symbolism of christmas trees

🎄 Evergreen trees are used for Christmas trees as a reminder of the everlasting life granted to us through Christ.

💡 The lights remind us that Christ is the light of the world.

🔴 The ornaments, originally red, remind us of the Tree of Life lost in the Garden of Eden and the new life given to us through Christ.

✨ 👼 On top of the tree sits a star as a reminder of the star that led the wise men to Jesus, or an angel reminding us of the angels sending the shepherds to Jesus.

👑 the epiphany

💡 An epiphany is a startling realization or discovery, as in the birth of Jesus, the Savior of the world.

🔭 The feast of the Epiphany celebrates the arrival of the three wise men to meet the baby Jesus.

🗺️ The three wise men from the East followed a star that led them to the newborn king. They brought gifts of

💰 gold,

🎵 frankincense,

🏺 and myrrh.

🎁 Many cultures give gifts on the Epiphany rather than on Christmas Day.

🐦 💧   The popular song about the twelve days of Christmas actually refers to the twelve days in between Christmas Day and the Epiphany.

🩶 ordinary time 🩶

The weeks in between the major seasons of Advent, Christmas, Lent, and Easter are in the season of Ordinary Time.

"Ordinary" doesn't mean boring or normal.

Ordinary refers to the Sundays being numbered in order:

1st Week in Ordinary Time

2nd Week in Ordinary Time

etc.

🌱 green is for growing

🩶 The liturgical color of Ordinary Time is green.

🌳 Green is the color of growing plants and nature.

🌱 We can think about Ordinary Time as a time for us to grow spiritually.

✅ ordinary time & jesus

The Gospel stories we hear during Ordinary Time focus on the ministry of Jesus:

📣 Preaching

🧑‍🏫 Teaching

☺ Healing

✧ Miracles

🩶 lent 🩶

Lent is a liturgical season of prayer and preparation for Easter.

For 40 days we fast, pray, and give to others as we journey with Jesus toward his passion, death, and resurrection.

Here is an introduction to Lent:

✚ ash wednesday ✚

Counting backwards from Easter Sunday by forty days (not counting the Sundays) we arrive at Ash Wednesday.

We wear ashes on our foreheads to remember our mortality.

We came from dust and to dust we will return.

📅 why forty days?

Forty is a significant number in the Bible. Each of these stories tell of people who go through a time of repentance and trial for forty days or years:

🚢 Noah & the Flood

🏜 Israelites Wander the Desert

🗻 Moses on Mt. Sinai

🏜 Jesus in the Desert

the three pillars of lent

During Lent we pray, fast, and give alms (charity).

These three spiritual practices help us to fight against temptation and become closer to God.

🍔 fish fridays

Why do we abstain from meat on Fridays during Lent (but eat fish instead)?

Historically:

🥩 was expensive

🐟 was cheap

Giving up meat was a way to give up luxury in solidarity with the poor.

It remains an opportunity to make a sacrifice on the day that Jesus died.

✝ stations of the cross ✝

The stations recall 14 moments during the crucifixion of Christ.

We walk along his same path of passion and death to humble ourselves and give thanks for his sacrifice for us.

✝ The Stations of the Cross with Emojis

I. 💀 Jesus Is Condemned to Death

We adore you, O Christ, and we bless you, because by your holy cross you have redeemed the world.

II. ✝ Jesus Takes Up the Cross

We adore you, O Christ, and we bless you, because by your holy cross you have redeemed the world.

III. 😔 Jesus Falls the First Time

We adore you, O Christ, and we bless you, because by your holy cross you have redeemed the world.

IV. 👫 Jesus Meets His Mother

We adore you, O Christ, and we bless you, because by your holy cross you have redeemed the world.

V. 🚶 Simon of Cyrene Helps Jesus Carry the Cross

We adore you, O Christ, and we bless you, because by your holy cross you have redeemed the world.

VI. 🧻 Veronica Wipes the Face of Jesus

We adore you, O Christ, and we bless you, because by your holy cross you have redeemed the world.

VII. 😖 Jesus Falls the Second Time

We adore you, O Christ, and we bless you, because by your holy cross you have redeemed the world.

VIII. 😢 Jesus Meets the Women of Jerusalem

We adore you, O Christ, and we bless you, because by your holy cross you have redeemed the world.

IX. 😣 Jesus Falls the Third Time

We adore you, O Christ, and we bless you, because by your holy cross you have redeemed the world.

X. 👕 Jesus Is Stripped of His Garments

We adore you, O Christ, and we bless you, because by your holy cross you have redeemed the world.

XI. 🔨 Jesus Is Nailed to the Cross

We adore you, O Christ, and we bless you, because by your holy cross you have redeemed the world.

XII. 😔 Jesus Dies on the Cross

We adore you, O Christ, and we bless you, because by your holy cross you have redeemed the world.

XIII. 🕊 Jesus's Body Is Taken Down from the Cross

We adore you, O Christ, and we bless you, because by your holy cross you have redeemed the world.

XIV. ⬇ Jesus Is Laid in the Tomb

We adore you, O Christ, and we bless you, because by your holy cross you have redeemed the world.

🙏 **Amen.**

💟 holy week 💟

Lent ends with a week of significant days at the height of the liturgical year.

🌿 Palm Sunday

🍞 Holy Thursday

✝ Good Friday

⬤ Holy Saturday

The final three days are called the Triduum.

Then . . .

☼ Easter Sunday!

🌅 easter 🌅

Easter is the celebration of the Resurrection of Jesus Christ.

🌅 The Meaning of Easter

📅 Easter: Day, Week, & Season

🕯 Easter Vigil

🙌 The Meaning of Alleluia

🕊 Ascension

🔥 Pentecost

🌅 the meaning of easter

"Easter" and "East" in English refer to the sunrise.

Most languages refer to Easter with the root word "Pasch" as in Paschal, which means Passover.

Jesus was celebrating Passover when he died and rose again.

Jesus started a new Passover.

📅 easter day, week, & season

📅 Day:

Easter Sunday celebrates the day of the Lord's Resurrection.

📅 Week:

The Easter Octave extends the celebration for 8 (octave) days.

📅 Season:

Easter lasts for 50 days from the Resurrection to Pentecost.

🕯 easter vigil

The Saturday night before Easter is the greatest celebration of the year.

- 🕯 Paschal Candle - blessed and used all year
- 😲 Exsultet - unique hymn about the Resurrection
- 📖 Long Liturgy of the Word: 16 readings total
- 💧 Sacraments of Initiation

🙌 the meaning of alleluia (hallelujah)

Alleluia means "praise Yahweh" or "praise God."

- 😶 We didn't say the A-word during Lent.
- 😲 During Easter we proclaim Alleluia constantly!

🌥 the ascension of the lord

⬆ 40 days after the Resurrection, Jesus ascended into heaven.

4 ☐ 0 ☐ 40 days after Easter (or the nearest Sunday) we celebrate the Ascension.

🙏 We remember that Jesus is in heaven, the Holy Spirit is with us, and he will come again.

🔥 pentecost

5 ☐ 0 ☐ Pentecost means 50.

🔥 50 days after the Resurrection, the Holy Spirit came upon the Apostles.

⬢ In the Old Testament, Pentecost celebrated God giving the Law.

❤ In the New Testament, Pentecost celebrates the Holy Spirit writing the Law on our hearts.

✍ author's note

🏃 This book began as a challenge.

✍ Could I write an entire book on my phone?

📱 If kids read and write in phone-sized keyboards, then what if I wrote a book that way?

🏛 I started writing Twitter (now X) threads about Catholic theology using my phone and emojis.

😊 And thus "theoloji" was born.

about the author

JARED DEES is the creator of The Religion Teacher (TheReligionTeacher.com), a popular website that provides practical resources and teaching strategies for religious educators. A respected graduate of the Alliance for Catholic Education (ACE) program at the University of Notre Dame, Dees holds master's degrees in education and theology, both from Notre Dame. He frequently gives keynotes and leads workshops at conferences, church events, and school in-services throughout the year on a variety of topics. He lives near South Bend, Indiana, with his wife and children.

Learn more about Jared's books, speaking events, and other projects at jareddees.com.

also by jared dees

- 31 Days to Becoming a Better Religious Educator
- To Heal, Proclaim, and Teach
- Christ in the Classroom
- Beatitales
- Tales of the Ten Commandments
- Do Not Be Afraid
- Take and Eat
- Pray without Ceasing
- Take Up Your Cross
- Prepare the Way
- Advent with the Angels
- 15-Minute Stations of the Cross for Kids
- The Angelus & Regina Caeli
- The Gospel According to Video Games
- Just Plant Seeds

📖 about thereligionteacher.com

TheReligionTeacher.com provides practical resources and teaching strategies for religious educators. Since Jared Dees founded The Religion Teacher in 2009, more than 100,000 catechists and religion teachers have signed up for the website's lesson plans, activities, worksheets, prayers, videos, and more.

📝 The Religion Teacher Member Resources

There are more than 1,000 downloadable worksheets and videos available to members of The Religion Teacher. To access these resources and opportunities for professional development, visit:

www.thereligionteacher.com